A wlw torture

Only mine, Never hers.

AF654706

Vaanika Arora

BlueRose ONE.com
Stories Matter
NewDelhi • London

BLUEROSE PUBLISHERS
India | U.K.

BlueRose ONE

For permissions requests or inquiries regarding this publication, please contact:

BLUEROSE PUBLISHERS
www.BlueRoseONE.com
info@bluerosepublishers.com
+91 8882 898 898
+4407342408967

ISBN: 978-93-7139-045-3

Cover Design: Aman Sharma
Typesetting: Pooja Sharma

First Edition: July 2025

DEDICATION

for all the girls who have mommy issues~

PREFACE

So, here's the thing - this book is kind of a mess of feelings. Like, way too much overthinking about a girl who probably didn't even notice most of it. But that's the point, right?

I didn't set out to write a perfect one-sided love story- because honestly, this isn't one. It's more like a scrapbook of what it feels like to be totally, hopelessly, maybe even a little bit crazy about a girl.

So, buckle up. It's going to be a wild, awkward ride where i wish i knew how to quit her.

PROLOGUE

Poem Bonus

She said we were just friends.
I said, "Okay."
But then she smiled like that.
Laughed like that.
Looked at me like maybe
Just...maybe
anddd.. she didn't mean it.

So I stayed. And wrote. And waited.

Call it obsession, call it delusion,
I call it heartache dressed in pretty texts and inside jokes.
Maybe she never wanted me.
Maybe she did.
But if love is a game,
I was always willing to lose,
as long as she kept playing.

FOREWORD

This is made of moments that never became more.
It's about longing that remained still,
and love that lived in *the in-between.*

Every poem is a little confession
of wanting, aching, waiting, hoping and choosing to stay
even when I shouldn't have.

And if she ever reads this,
which i'm pretty sure she will.
I'm not sorry for loving you.
It really was a privilege ;)

PLAYLIST

->blue
(Yung Kai)

->Sailor Song
(Gigi Perez)

->Stop Waiting
(cigarettes after sex)

->Summertime Sadness
(Lana Del Rey)

->Friends
(Chase Atlantic)

->Yellow
(Coldplay)

->i wanna be your girlfriend
(girl in red)

->Tum Ho
(Mohit Chauhan, Suzanne D'Mello)

->WILDFLOWER
(Billie Eilish)

->Reflections
(The Neighbourhood)

->Falling
(Trevor Daniel)

CONTENTS

POEM 1

I didn't need any reason to understand why I liked her,
It was a sensation that washed over me, gentle yet certain.

Then the shock hit- just friends until yesterday-
So why did it surprise me, this sudden realization,
What *a piece of art* she was, I couldn't quite put into words?

Damn, I'd developed *feelings.*

I fought them back as best I could,
but if I had kept them buried, I wouldn't have ever come to
write an entire book of poetries like this today.

POEM 2

i began to like her in the way you like someone when you're 13
and the world would still feel like it might crack open
if they just reciprocate your vibe.

we'd sit too close on the stairs at nights,
knees barely touching,
talking about nothing
like it mattered more than anything.

she had this way of making everything temporary feel infinite
like late-night walks to nowhere
or quiet meals across from each other
while she told me how she never wanted anything too permanent
because permanence felt like a trap.

and i said nothing,
because i didn't want to scare her off
with all the things I wanted to mean.

i think she liked being liked
but never wanted to hold it,
never wanted it to stick to her fingers
or turn into something that might
require showing up.

i liked her anyway.
a lot.
and maybe that was the whole problem.

POEM 3

Oh, I wonder how she was once just a face in the crowd,
Now, looking at her leaves my thoughts tangled.

She shifted from simple to a muse I can't escape,
My mind starts to overflow with poems every time,
wanting her more and more.

POEM 4

i'd never known calm until i saw her,
who smiled like she knew secret things
made room for the mess of everyone,
except maybe me.

POEM 5

Three years ago, I kinda barely remember,
just thought, "oh, okay, a senior."

But then something stuck-
her voice caught me off guard,
like it was quiet but full of something,
a little desperate, a little real,
and honestly, really attractive.

I don't know, I just really liked the way she sounded.
That voice? Yeah, it stayed with me.

POEM 6

Her long hair falling down, a golden cascade,
I watched in awe, mesmerized, afraid to invade.
We were sharing a cigarette,
The smoke swirled as she exhaled with a sigh,
Unaware as time passed by...

POEM 7

i like liking her-
like it's this wild wicked pain that won't quit,
like my heart's a drum beating too loud in my chest.

she doesn't have to try-
just blush like crimson is rushing to her cheeks,
flip her hair like she owns the world,
and i'm shattered and whole all at once.

it's stupid, it's messy,
but god, i'm addicted to this feeling-
the burning, the wanting,
the way just thinking about her makes me want to scream
and cry and,
write a gazillion poems.

i don't even need her back,
i just need this,
this terrible, beautiful wanting that makes me feel alive.

POEM 8

she's like the kind that walks into a room
and it shifts
not loud, not flashy
like the aura, just there.
like gravity,
like everyone suddenly remembers
they have eyes.

and maybe that's what i hated.
not her,
but *them.*
the way other girls looked at her
like she was mystery
they had the right to solve.
like they had a chance.

they didn't hear the way
she laughed when she tried for sleep to tug at her eyes
or the way she stared at ceilings
like they held answers.
they didn't know
how she'd run away from her own self when she's nervous
or how she once whispered
"i never thought i'd be this close to a junior."

others didn't feel it in their stomach
like hunger, like heat,
like *please, just once, look at me like that.*

if girls didn't fall for her
they were either blind
or straight.
or maybe lucky.
because loving her
felt like drowning
and still refusing to come up for air.

POEM 9

She was unapologetically her, with innocence in her eyes,
And I didn't fall in love, *I flew*.

Each moment with her felt like a breath of wild, surreal air,
Her spirit lifted mine, without a single care.
In her presence, I was free, caught in a love soooo rare.

POEM 10

i want to tell her she's beautiful
in a "i look at you and forget how to act" way.

i check her posts too much.
i replay her voice in my head.
i overthink every second she gives me.

i'm scared people will say it's a phase
and i'm being weak
or that i'm being dramatic
but no.
she's the one i think about
every time someone says "who do you like."

i don't want the world to see this
but i want her to
just her. just once.

it's that simple. it's that complicated.

i don't understand why I like her so much
there's no reason, no logic.
still, I hold on, even when it hurts,
because letting go feels impossible.

POEM 11

We simply shared moments,
yet something began to grow.

Her laugh, her touch,
pulling me closer, so sensitively.
in every glance, a secret I couldn't hide,
falling for her, though she kept her feelings tied.

I searched for answers in the quiet we'd keep,
wondering if she felt the same,
or if it was just for me to steep.

POEM 12

she once said
"i've always been the listener"
like it was just a fact
like her voice was never meant to take up space
but somehow, with me,
she can't stop talking.

and oh lord
do you know what that girl does to me?
watching her words spill out
like she feels safe here,
like i'm the silence she trusts enough to break.

i don't even need to speak.
i just sit there, watching her lips move,
thinking
if this is what loving her feels like-
so full and endlessly mellow
then maybe i never want the talking to end.

POEM 13

once was the time
september, october
when i was indulged
in something that called itself a situationship.
a guy.
just a noise to fill the space
i didn't want to name.

and she
she was everywhere.
searching for me in every dorm,
holding conversations like they were lost coins,
waiting every day
just to hear *me.*

and i?
i was stupid.
or scared.
or both.
because she was seeing somebody else,
and i wasn't ready to call this
what it was.

so i kept talking to him.
pretending i wanted something simple
when what i craved
was *her.*

but she never knew.
never knew i stopped texting him

sometime in october.
never knew i ghosted him
without explanation
because i realized
i liked her too much,
too much to even *make time*
to think about anyone else.

and by then,
november, december,
she was already slipping.
caught in the rush of passing out,
finishing school,
moving on.
busy in ways i should've seen coming.

i lost the version of her
that had once been all mine for a while
without even knowing it.

and now i wait.
for a message,
for a moment,
for *her*
to come back like the girl from september.

because if she ever does,
i swear-
i'll tell her this time.
i'll say it out loud:

i crave her lesbianism
like it's religion.
like it's oxygen.
like it's everything
i tried so hard not to want
until wanting her
was all i knew how to do.

POEM 14

she said
"I never thought of being this close to a junior yk,"
like it slipped out,
like it surprised even her.

& i laughed
but inside i felt my intestine
turn into a thousand fireflies.

i know she missed her senior too.
her ex. the one she still texts.
the one i never minded
but maybe that's a lie.
maybe i did. just a little.

because i sit there wondering
if she ever looks at me
like i look at her.

i wonder if she thinks of me
when we both fall silent
& the night hums between us.
or when we talk about futures
& somehow, we imagine
the same kinds of things
even the secret ones
we *only whisper.*

it was always easy with her.
like our minds knew the same rhythm

our hearts practiced the same ache
& somehow our ideas of touch
aligned without us planning it.

i don't know if we'd work out
but i dream about it anyway.
like maybe one day,
she'll say that thing again
but mean it a little differently
like maybe she wants to stay.

POEM 15

her head leaned on my knee,
what was i supposed to do with that?

maybe she liked the way i saw her
the quiet corners she rarely showed.
maybe that was enough for her.
to be seen.
to be held in someone's attention
without having to hold anything back.

i think she liked being close,
but not too close.
liked me around,
but not enough to stay.

so did she like me back?
maybe...
maybe just enough to keep me wondering,
but not enough to make it real.
not enough to choose it.
and maybe that's the kind of answer
you never really get
just the silence after they leave
and don't look back.

POEM 16

i asked her once,
shy-ly, almost joking
"have you ever been attracted to me?"

and she-
oh god-

she blushed.
nodded.

eyes all unsure
like she wasn't used to being seen
like that.

and me?
i froze.
panicked.
laughed too loud.
said something stupid like,
"ohh i just ask that to every girl...haha..."

every girl??
god. i barely used to talk to any-
she looked away.
and i saw it
that flicker in her.
like she was folding herself
back into the "not-special" box
i had accidentally made for her.

but she's not.
she's not one of many.
she's not a joke i toss around
to hear myself laugh.

she's the one
i didn't plan on falling for
but somehow,
it happened before i could even notice.

POEM 17

what she didn't know
is that question
was a hint.
a nervous little thread
i was trying to hand her
because i was too scared
to hand her my whole heart.

i was already too deep.
already too attached
to the way she just... *is.*

that wasn't a game.
it wasn't a bit.
it was me saying,
i want you so bad it scares me,
without actually saying it.

someone, tell her.
tell her i only asked
because i already knew
what my heart was doing.

that it wasn't just a random question
it was the only one that mattered.
& i messed it up
with a laugh
when i should've said

yes.
you.
it's you.
only you.

POEM 18

she'd laugh,
tilt her head like nothing was serious,
say something like
"you always read too much into things,"
whenever i got too quiet,
or my cheeks gave me away
before my mouth could lie.

but *she knew.*
she knew when she leaned in close
and i stopped breathing.

she knew when her fingers brushed mine
and i flinched
not from fear,
but from everything.

she knew the moment she said
"you ask every girl that, right?"
and i laughed too quickly.
she knew
that my laugh was a cover
and my throat was internally screaming.

i know she was never oblivious.
she was just kind.
too kind to break me open
before i was ready to bleed.

POEM 19

she felt it.
the way I looked at her,
the way my voice softened when i said her name.

she knew.
she knew i wanted her,
not in a fleeting, crush-kind-of-way,
but in that terrifying way
you want someone to choose you back.

and still-
still, she held back.
like she'd already decided
there was no point.

so I started to believe her.
i told myself it was all in my head.
that maybe I made it up
that maybe I was the only one feeling anything at all.

but the truth is,
i wasn't just feeling something.
i was falling.
hard and fast
into her.
and in trying not to chase her,
i started losing parts of myself
she never even asked for.

POEM 20

I feel this urge to heal her, to mend what's torn,
To show her the beauty she can't see, what her true worth is.
I write these words, hoping one day she'll read,
And realize she's everything, more than she'd ever need.

She's deserving of love, of things she's yet to understand,
A truth I see clearly, though it slips right through her hands.

Though she thinks I'm just another girl- oblivious and madly in love,
I just want her to know, I don't look at her like the ones she's surrounded by,
For in my eyes, she's a world apart, a universe all on her own,
And I see her for who she really is, not who they've all grown.

POEM 21

I made a lot of moves, knowing she's noticing,
Oh, the doe eyes I always got from her.
Each glance of hers deepened the pull,
My feelings began to develop more,
But with each passing moment,
I understood I would never share a single one with her, ever.

POEM 22

I guess she was too shy to voice it,
but I convinced myself she felt the same.
I held onto hope, clinging to a dream that kept me awake.
I waited for a love from her that never came,
and in the end, I was left facing the truth-
That it was a love only I carried.

But of course, I didn't stop trying again
I'm so dumb, I'd beg the same tranquility to speak.

POEM 23

i wanted to be her favorite
the arms she'd fall into
when the world got too loud.
but something was always off.
like i came in with the wrong story
or too much want.

she was twelve steps ahead,
a year above,
a life above,
and i was just sixteen and spilling over.

it's stupid how much she lives in those roads,
we once walked together at.
lives in my head,
during math,
during lights-out,
even in the middle of brushing my teeth.

i can't study without her name
ghosting every word.
still...
i'm learning the language of her,
hoping she lets me in someday.

POEM 24

she never came to me,
not really
but she never left my mind either.

like a song stuck on repeat,
a 'haunting' that felt *too warm* to forget.

and maybe that was enough
holding her there,
even if she was never close enough to touch.

POEM 25

I started questioning if she ever cared,
wondering if those quiet moments meant anything to her.
But the more I thought about it,
the more resentment crept in
though how could I ever hate her?
She was too easy to love,
too genuine in everything she did.
I wanted to be angry,
but she never asked for any of this,
never meant for me to feel this way.
I hated that, in the end,
loving her had never been a choice.

POEM 26

She was too much in her head, lost in thoughts that ran deep,
And I wanted to lift her from dreams.
wanted to try to show her a love that could heal every scar,
to remind her she's worth it, no matter how far.

But she built walls I couldn't tear down,
And I understood, love can't heal what's not willing to be found.

POEM 27

Her eyes searched for love, and I felt it deep within,
I yearned to give it, give to the place where I thought I fit in.
But somehow, she always pushed me away, making me feel
I'd never win.

But in my mind, I, everyday, won the love,
It kept me going as it was only me I could trust.

After all, as they say-
"one-sided love holds the most power,
not even the whole universe dares to resist its force."
Because wanting alone can carry worlds,
and I carried her in all of mine.

POEM 28

I wrote my truth, a susurration on paper,
An adrenaline rush in my chest, a feeling untamed,
That gut squeeze I can't explain,
I believed I could wait till I didn't have to,
In her embrace, to find my place.

She never properly replied, instead, she slipped away,
distance grew, not in words but in space,
And I kept hoping, waiting for a sign.

POEM 29

we can never be together,
she made that clear
with every gentle no,
like i should be grateful
for the ache.

she says she doesn't wanna ruin
what we have,
but what is it we have
if *not something already cracked,*
held together by me pretending it's enough?

this bridge is thin,
and i'm the only one walking.
she waves from the edge,
turn back to safer ground,
while i wait
stuck between her distant hush
and all the things
i wish she'd say.

POEM 30

all of it was one-sided, of course,
a love I held, but she would never ever feel.

something kept me anchored, waiting patiently, believing with faith,
in a dream that was mine, but never took its place...
i always thought she gave me hints,
like there was something unspoken, a truth to define.

but something seemed to always hold her back,
made her stay still,
or maybe it was just me,
lost in what I wished to feel.

POEM 31

I watch her face,
The way her eyes light up when she's near.
But the second she looks away, I *ache*,
Missing the warmth she didn't mean to break.

Eyes spoke what the mouth couldn't say,
A silent connection that blew me away.
In that brief moment, everything else disappeared.

POEM 32

she was mine only in my mind, and that had to be enough,
while she laughed like nothing was true.
now I can't even want her for real
i've loved the version only I knew.

she's right there but not with me
i keep thinking she'll say something she won't
i make up moments that aren't real
though both the world and I understand,
the real her will never be mine.

POEM 33

and i can't even blame her.
not really.
she never promised me anything,
never asked me to wait.

i filled in the blanks myself.
read between lines that were never written.
i created a whole story
from the empty spaces she left between us
i made her into something more than she was
someone who *could've* been everything,
if only the timing had been right,
if only i hadn't loved her from the edges,
waiting for a connection she never intended to make.

POEM 34

she keeps on asking
why i'm so nice to her
like it's some kind of mystery.

but ugh
does she really not get it?
i *chose* her.
i don't do this for just anyone.

i don't forgive like this.
i don't stay like this.
not unless it's *her*.

and yeah,
it hurts like hell.
i tell myself to stop,
to walk away.
but something in me
won't let go.

it drags me back every time.
and i hate it.
but i hate not having her more.

POEM 35

My head holds the weight of months without a word,
A hollow pain, too raw to be voiced.
Maybe if we'd figured things out sooner... maybe if we'd just talked, really talked...
I keep replaying everything in my head, wondering if I messed it all up.

Did I say the wrong thing?
Miss the signs?
I don't know.
I just wish we'd had the chance to become something more.

POEM 36

i've learned how to fold myself
into the corners of her life.
not center,
not spotlight
but there.
just for a while,
where i console myself that it's enough.

she says i'm her closest,
a friend like no other.
not what i want,
but almost.

and?? i stay
because she's happy when i do.

it's fine, i tell myself,
as long as she's happy.
even if it means
being a prisoner
to the feelings of my own
that won't go away.

POEM 37

Thinking of her always unsettled me.

I looked for her in others
the way someone tucks their hair behind an ear
and for a moment, I pretend.
I let myself believe
this one might make me forget.
But it never lasts.

They're not her.
They never are.

And I hate how I try
to stitch pieces of strangers together
just to feel close to someone
who's already gone.

All I want is her
not a reflection, not a copy
just her,
the way she was when she looked at me
like I meant something.

POEM 38

The ones who cared
they said, and I could hardly believe
how I'd mirrored her with myself towards them
without ever meaning to.

I lost good friends along the way,
too busy bleeding for someone
who barely saw me there.

I watched them fade without a word,
while I held fast to reverberations,
loving someone who never loved me back,
and didn't see the ones who held out their hands.

POEM 39

My devotion to her so deep,
A language of love she never consoled.
Her heart distant, cold,
Yet yearning for her, mine stayed warm.

I was in love with her, all in my head,
Afraid to face her worth once she was gone, instead.
Thank goodness I liked her then, for now, I know I can't anymore.

POEM 40

I don’t know how to love,
or maybe I thought I didn’t.
But when it was her,
everything I believed in just faded.

I tried to defy,
tried to hold onto my rules,
but with her,
love wasn’t a question,
it was a flame I couldn't put out.

All the things I believed in,
the things that kept me safe,
they slipped away
the moment she smiled at me.

And suddenly,
I wasn’t sure anymore
what I was guarding,
or why I thought I had control.

With her,
I was crashing down,
and I didn’t know how to stop.

POEM 41

Living in that grey space,
she kept me close enough to feel wanted,
but far enough to stay untouched.
and *i let her.*
god, i let her.

POEM 42

when we have to say goodbye
after every call, every laugh, every *stolen moment*
is like tearing a piece of myself away.

the words stick in my throat,
the silence screams louder than anything we said,
knowing that with each goodbye,
she slips just a little further out of reach.

i want to hold on,
to freeze time,
to swallow the pain and never let go
but i have to let her go.

and that's the cruelest part:
knowing that no matter how many times i say goodbye,
it's never really over
because she stays,
she just always does.

POEM 43

she doesn't try to fix things,
but somehow, she does.
in the way she listens,
in the way she stays
when i expect everyone to leave.

she remembers little things
and it makes something unfamiliar
settle in me.

i never called it missing
until she filled the quiet
my mother left behind.

and now,
i crave that kind of presence
more than i ever meant to.
it makes me angry,
how much it matters,
how much *she* does.

POEM 44

i don't want anything from her.
not her love, not her words,
not even a moment-
especially not if she's not ready to offer it.

i just want her to breathe
without the weight of my feelings on her shoulders.
i want her to know
i'm not keeping score.

she doesn't owe me a thing.
not a kiss, not a glance,
not even the closure i sometimes crave.

because in my eyes,
even the way she once looked at me
like i mattered-
that was everything.

so no,
i don't need her to love me back.
i just need her to never carry guilt
for something she never asked me to feel.

POEM 45

she's out of this place now
but somehow we still talk
call, text, flirt
or maybe it's just me
but god, the way she blushes
when i say things i shouldn't say out loud
like i want her in ways
girls aren't supposed to want *girls.*

she hides her face,
like she wants this
but something bigger holds her back.
and i keep waiting
not for her,
but for the moment she lets herself want me too.

POEM 46

i message her
even when the conversation's empty.
she's back home,
counting down to august and college,
while i sit in class
with her stuck in my head.

we talk more now
than we ever did
when we actually had time.
she says silly things like
"*i miss youuuu*"
and somehow all those extra letters
feel like they matter.
and again. shit. i laugh more than i should.

my face goes hot.
my hands go cold.
i know i could move on.
but i don't want to.
something in me
just wants to stay.

POEM 47

i see it in her
the way joy dances on her face
only to retreat
like a tide too hesitant to stay.

she doesn't completely shut me out,
but i can feel the doors close
around her guard,
like she's saving us both
from what we might become.

she laughs,
then folds into worldless pauses,
not cold, just careful.
as if loving me
would be too expensive to lose.

maybe she's right.
maybe we're two hands
gripping something so fragile,
Too uncertain to hold tighter
in case it breaks.

so we settle
for eye contact that lingers,
for words that almost say it,
for a friendship
standing at the threshold
of everything we won't admit.

POEM 48

She had cut one string in my heart with love,
The rest unraveled, but in the best way,
Each thread of tender ecstasy led me to stay.
Her love had *shattered* me,
in the most beautiful way.

POEM 49

she's one of a kind,
that makes me want to scream...
just to prove i saw her first.

i'd wear her name like armor,
fight like hell for her peace.
swear vengeance on every name
that ever made her cry.

she laughs and the world shifts.
she hurts and i burn mutely.

but....
i hope she's not the kind
to pocket all my care
and leave me looking like being too easy to love.

i'm not scared of loving her.
i'm scared of what happens
if it was never real for her
the way it is for me.

POEM 50

she laughs at things no one else finds funny,
and somehow, i laugh too.

she trips on her own feet,
loses track of her own sentence.
she's dumb. Truly.
but i like her.
which probably makes me worse.
because i see it all,
and still fall harder every time.

she gets into trouble
with no way out,
but laughs like it's no big deal
like getting stuck is just her thing.

maybe love is just
being silly together,
and not caring
who fell first
as long as we both did.

EPILOGUE

she once told me,
when i asked
how many poems should be in a book.
she said:
"fifty."

but this is the 51st.
because she isn't here
and i am.
and maybe that's unfair
or maybe that's fate
or maybe it's just high school ending
without her in this place.

but i need her to know
if she has ever thought love could be measured
in pages,
or poems,
or delayed communications,
she was wrong
and i'm not mad that she was.
she always tried to stay within the lines
even when her heart didn't want to.

so here's the thing:
i never wanted a minimum with her.
not fifty, not even one.
i wanted all of them.
every stray poem,

every look she thought i didn’t notice,
every version of hers
in every life we don’t get to live.

this 51st one
is not the end.
it’s me saying
if fate finds us again,
she doesn't have to hold back.
she doesn't have to shrink her wants
until they fit neat on a shelf.

go past the fifty,
past the silence,
past the goodbye
she never wanted to say.

i’ll be waiting
still writing,
still not counting.

-yours, truly.

ACKNOWLEDGEMENT

To my school gang-

Thank you for always being braced with comfort whenever I started yapping about her. Whether you were listening through silence, or threatening to spill everything on me the moment I did something dumb(again), you made the chaos feel lighter.

To Kay,
For always pushing me to go get hurt, because how else would I have known she was right all along?

To Sid and Bans,
The tireless pigeons, running back and forth with sticky notes and messages.
never once complaining, even when it wasn't their mess to carry.

To Aps,
Who never hesitated to hit me with reality checks, especially when I said the dumbest things with too much confidence.

To Zoe,
An aromantic who listened to every tangled detail about her, and roasted me with unforgettable precision.

To Prats and Shell,
Always visibly annoyed with all the 'her' talk, i knew they both were two seconds away from punching me, but they still stayed. still listened. every single time.

I couldn't have survived all that overthinking without your background commentary, or your emotional support which made it all bearable. Thank you bbgs<3.

ABOUT THE AUTHOR

Vaanika Arora is sixteen, and *Only Mine, Never Hers* is her first book. She wrote it because some memories, especially the ones about *her*, just wouldn't leave her alone. Writing became her way of saying what she couldn't out loud. She thinks that some stories can be kept hidden for a while, but eventually, at a point, she believes that they need to be heard.

She admits she may have forced herself to publish it, partly due to her own inner pressure, partly because holding it in had started to feel heavier than letting it out. These poems were born from a private nook she rarely speaks from, somewhere between silence and survival.

Writing about *her*, the way she stays, listens, simply exists, helped Vaanika shift from reacting to reflecting. In telling this story, she always found a strange kind of healing. *She* made her want to be more *patient* with the parts of herself she'd once learned to hate.

This book isn't just about love or loss- it's about learning to live with both.